And we sailed the

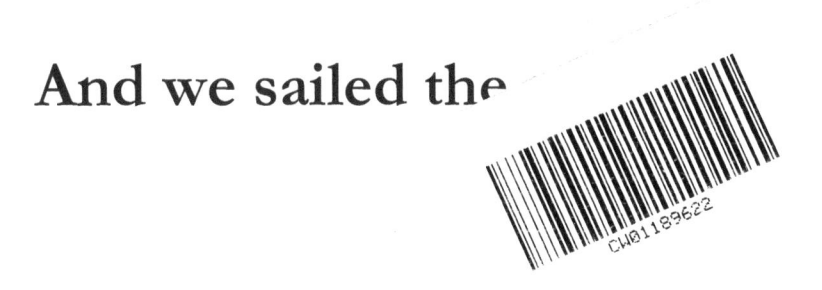

Frank Belknap Long

Alpha Editions

This edition published in 2024

ISBN : 9789366382449

Design and Setting By
Alpha Editions
www.alphaedis.com
Email - info@alphaedis.com

As per information held with us this book is in Public Domain.
This book is a reproduction of an important historical work. Alpha Editions uses the best technology to reproduce historical work in the same manner it was first published to preserve its original nature. Any marks or number seen are left intentionally to preserve its true form.

Contents

CHAPTER I ....- 1 -
CHAPTER II ....- 7 -
CHAPTER III ....- 13 -
CHAPTER IV ....- 21 -

CHAPTER I

Graveyard of Old Ships

You've seen them—the old ships, the battered and ruined ships, the ships that have made one voyage too many, and are so ancient you can't remember their names or the reputations they've earned for themselves in deep space! Sure you've seen them! Black hulls stretching away for miles into the red sunset—ships that can be bought for a song if you've a song left in you and still want to go adventuring on the rim of the System.

Do you know how it feels not to have a song left in you? Do you know how it feels to be a legend without substance—the lad who broke the bank at Callisto City and walked out two days later without a penny to his name?

Pete knew and he kept harping on it. "If you'd quit that first night, Jim, instead of pushin' it all back across the board!"

There was awe in his eyes when he looked at me, and then he'd look at the ships, and I could guess what he was thinking. Good old Pete! When he shut his eyes I was still wearing a golden halo.

Lucky Jim Sanders, strong as an ox and coming along fine—born lucky and loving life too much to worry his head about the future. But when life rises up and wallops you and lays you out flat you forget the good times and your own recklessness, and the inner strength and the laughing girls, and you just want to sit down and never get up!

I'd met Pete down in the valley, sitting on a rock. He didn't want to get up either. He wanted to croak.

A wiry little cuss with blue eyes and a fringe of beard on his chin that had just grown there and stayed. Clothes that made him look like he was trying to spin a cocoon about himself.

You bet he had a story! A hard luck story that would have made Sinbad look like a quiet family man. But when I like someone straight off, his past is just so much water over the dam if he wants it that way.

I never did find out the truth about Pete—right up until we parted. I had a lot of fun kidding him about it. "Rip Van Winkle slept twenty years, but you slept a thousand, Pete! You crawled out of an old ship and went to sleep in the desert.

"Did you get tired, Pete? Of the roar and the dust and the night—the crocus-flower faces of Venusians, the gopher-girls of Mars and the pinwheeling stars—of the night and the dust and the roar? Couldn't you take it in the old days, Pete, when ships kept bursting apart at the seams and there was an ant hill on Callisto called a colony, with twenty living dead men in it?

"The ant hill's a city now, Pete. And you're still Pete, still around, and I'm just cutting my wisdom teeth on my first streak of hard luck! Hard like a biscuit, Pete! A dog biscuit flung to a dog!"

I was raving even more wildly as I stared out over that graveyard of old ships, feeling sorry for myself, envying Pete because he didn't seem to care much whether he lived or died.

But I was wrong. Pete did care.

"If we could just get back to Earth, Jim!" he pleaded. "If we could smell the green earth again, after it's been rainin'! If we could just get a whiff o' the sea!"

I swung on him. "What chance have we? You don't value dough so much when you've got it to toss around. But when you're stony broke you get to feeling like a stone. Weighed down, petrified! You can't do anything without dough!"

Pete made a clucking sound. "All right! You got trimmed, Jim—and bad! But last night you had another streak of luck!"

I stared at him, hard.

He gestured toward the old ships. "There's a yardmaster down there with a list of ships a yard long. If you want to buy a ship you just stand around twiddling your thumbs until he notices you. If he sizes you up right—you get a bargain!"

"You mean if he thinks you've got some dough, but not much?"

"Uh huh!" Pete winked. "But if he thinks you've got a lot of dough you could get a bargain too. Without shelling out a cent!"

It didn't take me long to get what Pete was driving at. I'd taken a beating, and everyone knew it. But everyone knew my face too! I was still Lucky Jim Sanders, wearing a golden halo!

Pete's eyes were shining like Halley's Comet when I got through coaching him. It was his idea, but when I tossed it back at him wrapped up in dialogue the sparkle took his breath away!

We went down into the valley where the ships stood row on row, shouting and reeling as though we'd been celebrating for a week. The yardmaster heard us before he saw us. But he saw us quickly enough.

His lips tightened as he came striding toward us—a bushy-browed, hard-bitten old barnacle with a crusty stare. I could tell the exact instant when he recognized me. His jaw dropped about six inches; then closed with a click.

"Now!" I whispered to Pete.

Pete raised his voice. "You're higher than a kite!" he shouted. "Why buy a flying coffin when you could own the sweetest little job in the System?"

"What I do with my dough is my own business!" I shouted back. "They knew how to build ships in the old days!"

"I tell you—you're crazier than a diving loon!"

"Sure I'm crazy!" I agreed. "Only a baby with curvature of the brain could win back a cool eighty thousand on one spin of the wheel! But I'm sane enough not to want to thin out my take!"

"You'd flip a coin for one o' those flyin' coffins?"

"Why not?" I roared belligerently. "I've got five thousand that says I know what I'm doing! Five thousand against—the right to pick my own ship!"

I tripped myself then, deliberately by accident. I went sprawling over Pete's out-thrust right leg. When I picked myself up I must have looked as helpless as a new-born babe, because the yardmaster was gripping my arm and refusing to let go.

"You were saying, mister?"

He was seeing the halo, of course, the rim of gold about my head. I was pretty sure he wouldn't even ask me to cover my bet.

The copper piece on my palm seemed to fascinate him. He couldn't take his eyes from it.

"What will it be?" I asked.

He swallowed hard. "Heads!" he said.

I flipped the coin.

"Tails it is!" I told him.

He stared at my palm suspiciously. I grinned and handed him the copper piece. There was nothing wrong with it.

"I never cheat!" I said.

I walked over to where she stood collecting rust in the red Jupiterlight—the ship I'd picked out. She wasn't so ancient as old ships go. She must have been built around 2097, just a hundred years before I'd won her. We were riding hard on your luck!

"Got a navigator's license?" the yardmaster asked.

"Sure! Want to see it?"

He shook his head. "Never mind! Take her and get going before I start telling myself I'm the System's prize sap!"

The control room was as musty as a tomb, and when I switched on the cold lights our shadows looked like black widow spiders dangling from the overhead.

"She'll never hold together!" Pete groaned.

"Don't be like that!" I chided. "All of these ships have to pass a rigid inspection."

Pete blinked. "You sure of that?"

"Well ... maybe the inspectors skip a ship here and there," I conceded.

I went over her from stem to stern, to make sure she wouldn't fly about when I gave her the gun. While I inspected the atomotors Pete kept giving me uneasy looks, like he was dying to ask me where I'd picked up my knowledge of ghost ships, but was scared I'd say something to shake his confidence in me.

I wasn't worried. I can be awfully sure of myself when I'm around anything mechanical, from an inch-high rheostat to the guide lines on a sixty-foot control board.

The ship had the right feel about her. I'd have trusted my life to her, but Pete kept sniffing like he could smell the odor of charred flesh. To make him feel better I thumped him on the back and told him not to worry, that he'd appreciate what a fine ship she was when he saw the green Earth filling the viewpane, misty with spring rains. He'd lived alone so long he'd become suspicious of everything.

Eaten up by his own fears, tormented by shadows, an old man before his time. Some of my confidence seemed to seep into him as I talked. He didn't look so old when he looked up.

He was sitting on a bulkhead chronometer, which meant that time was ticking away right under him. He was a dead ringer for old Father Time himself, but for an instant as he returned my stare there was a strange look in his eyes. As though he'd shrugged off his woes, and was gazing straight back across the years at his lost youth.

"Maybe you're right, Jim," he said. "When do we take off?"

"Before the yardmaster visiphones Callisto City to find out if I really did make a killing last night!" I told him.

I was standing close to the control board, my thumb on the oscillatory circuit. There are two ways of starting an atomotor. You can test out the strength of the circuit by letting the power drum through the board before you give the dial a full turn.

Or you can switch the power on full blast, reaching peak in ten seconds and letting the ship do its own testing. I liked the second way best. A ship that can't absorb the shock of a take-off at sixty gravities will almost certainly fly apart in space.

I switched the power on full strength. From the corner of one eye I had a brief, soul-satisfying glimpse of Pete stiffening in utter consternation. A mean trick to play on a pal? No. I don't think so. I wasn't asking him to take the plunge alone. I was sharing the risks, and I was doing him a favor.

When you're taking a swim you just prolong the agony by sitting around on a diving raft wriggling your toes in the icy water. It's best to jump right in, and get it over with.

We must have been twenty thousand feet up when Pete's startled face slipped out of focus, and I found myself on my hands and knees on a deck that was revolving like a centrifuge. Cathode rays were darting in all directions, and everything in the path of the rays glowed with fluorescent light. I knew that the ship was X-raying itself while fog condensed on the negative ions of its hull and dissolved into sizzling steam.

I didn't try to get up immediately. I waited for the deck to stop gyrating and the strength to return to my wrists. My right arm was numb and tingling. When I raised my hands I could see the bones in my fingers. All pilots have skeleton hands when they take off. It's a second-order cathode ray effect which vanishes after a minute or two. It doesn't mean a thing. Not if you're sound of mind and limb, and the ship you've picked is spaceworthy.

But Pete seemed to take a different view. He was staring at me in horror. I knew what he was thinking. If I was pinch-hitting for Death—I'd got off to a good start.

He, too, was on his knees on the deck, his shoulders swaying, his face turned toward me in bitter reproach.

Suddenly his eyes blazed with anger. "Son, I ought to get up and bust you one on the jaw! If you'd warned me, I could have braced myself!"

I hadn't thought of that. But before I could tell him how sorry I felt, he was chuckling!

"It's all right, Jim! No bones broken! She sure took it beautifully, eh?"

"She sure did!" I muttered.

I watched him get to his feet and go reeling toward the viewpane. Mr. Chameleon was the name for him! He could change his moods so fast, his mental outlook must have been as dazzling as a display of fireworks.

A guy like that just couldn't hold a grudge. If you poked him in the ribs he'd blacken your eye and give you his last ounce of tobacco. Good old Pete! Insatiably curious he was too, like a little boy at a circus side show.

He just couldn't wait to see how far up we were, had to look out the viewpane before his brain stopped spinning.

I was satisfied just to sit on the deck and watch him.

For an instant he stared out, his face pressed to the pane, the pulse in his forehead swelling visibly.

Then, abruptly, he turned and flashed me a startled look. "Jehoshaphat, Jim! We—we can't be travelin' that fast! Callisto's just a little crawlin' red gnat in the middle o' the sky!"

CHAPTER II

Planet Shift

I stared at him uneasily. He was talking like an idiot. I knew that Jupiter itself would have to dwindle to a small disk before Callisto could become a pin point of light. When you take off from a little moon the glare of its primary magnifies its surface features. For about one hour Callisto would look like a black orchid dwindling in a blaze of light. Then it would whip away into emptiness to reappear as a glowing dot.

"Jupiter looks funny too!" Pete muttered. "Mighty funny! Like a big slice o' yellow cheese with golden bands around it, spreadin' out—"

That did it! I got up and walked to the viewpane, slapping my hands together explosively. I had to let off steam in some way. My steadiness surprised me. My eyelids felt a little heavy, but there was nothing wrong with my space legs.

When I started out I didn't see the red gnat. But I saw something else, something that gave me a tremendous shock. What I saw was a great ringed planet swimming in a golden haze!

When I turned my face must have given Pete a jolt. He gulped so hard I was afraid he'd swallow his Adam's apple and choke on the rind.

"What is it, Jim?" he asked huskily. "You look like you'd seen a ghost!"

I laughed without amusement. "I did! A ghost planet! And we're not moving away from it! It's getting larger!"

Pete stared. "Sure you feel okay, son?"

"Not too good!" I said, looking him straight in the eye. "Take another look!"

I gestured toward the viewpane. "Go on! See for yourself!"

Pete stood for a long time with his face pressed to the pane, his shoulders hunched. I thought he was never going to turn.

A crazy thought flashed through my mind. I'd seen men in a state of collapse on their feet, their faces blanched, unable to move or speak. Had Pete been shocked speechless?

I was sweating as he turned. His face was blanched, all right, but he could speak, and did!

"I've got to sit down, Jim!" he choked out.

He reeled to the bulkhead chronometer, sat down and started tugging at his chin. After a moment he whipped his hand from his face.

"You're an educated man, Jim," he said. "I'm not! If you tell me we're headin' straight for Saturn, I won't call you a liar!"

"You won't?"

"No, Jim. Say a guy brings you a watch. The hands go in the wrong direction, the tickin's so loud it drives you nuts. 'Buddy,' he says, 'if you want to know what time it isn't, this watch will tell you.'

"Well, say you've got to know the time, say your life depends on it. What do you do, Jim? Lift him up by his seat and toss him out the door? Shucks, no! You listen while he talks. You ask him to take the watch apart and show you what makes it tick."

"Fine!" I said. "So I'm the man with the watch! I put Saturn outside the viewpane just to torture you!"

He looked so miserable I felt sorry for him. "I didn't mean it that way, Jim," he apologized. "But I'm plumb scared! Somethin's happenin' to space! Somethin' ghastly awful! You must have some idea what's causin' it!"

"Don't kid yourself!" I told him. "A wild guess isn't an idea."

"Let me be the judge o' that, son!"

"Well—all right. Maybe we're seeing Saturn as a magnified image—through some kind of magnifying space drift. A big, floating lens in space, made up of refractive particles spread out in a cloud. A lens with more magnifying power than the five-hundred inch! It isn't as haywire as it sounds, if that's any comfort to you!"

"But no pilot's ever seen anything like that, Jim!" Pete protested, with unanswerable logic.

He tapped his brow. "It could be in here, Jim! That's what I'm afraid of! A sickness of the mind—"

"Don't start that!" I warned, striking my knee with my fist. "Don't even think it!"

My voice was getting out of control. I was yelling at him, and there was no reason for it.

He had every right to his opinion.

"What are we goin' to do, Jim?"

"Check up first!" I snapped. "If I have to use every instrument on the ship—"

I stopped. The door into the pilot room had opened and closed, and a clumping figure was coming toward us across the deck.

I heard Pete suck in his breath. I couldn't seem to draw a deep breath. There was a physical quality of eeriness in the sight which took me by the throat.

The figure was wearing a light spacesuit, vacuum-sealed at the neck. A transparent headpiece bulged out above the flexible garment, a great glistening globe encasing the head of the most beautiful woman I'd ever seen.

Her hair was piled in a tumbled mass of gold on her head and there was a delicate flush on her skin, visible through the glowing sphere. She was staring at me without seeming to see me, her cheeks shadowed by long, convex lashes.

Some women mature into loveliness; others have it thrust upon them. I didn't tell myself that straight off. I was too stunned to make up pretty speeches. But later I realized that her hair, eyes, and complexion were as near perfect as they could be without looking artificial.

Her suit was cumbersome, and it weighed her down. But there was something weird, spine-chilling about the way she moved. She walked with a smooth flow of motion, almost as if she were skating across the deck.

I was a little afraid of what Pete might do. He was shaking with excitement, and I could see that he was keyed up to a dangerous pitch. Doubting his own sanity and mine to boot!

But I wasn't going to be stampeded into fear! I'd been under a tremendous strain, sure. But I knew a flesh-and-blood woman when I saw one! The girl was real! The pulse beating in her forehead was real and so were her eyes and hair! We hadn't made even a cursory search of the ship. There were plenty of dark little corners where she could have concealed herself.

Suddenly I saw that she'd glided past Pete and was facing away from us, her hands extended toward the control board. A little to the left of the board there was a dull flickering on the bulkhead.

For an instant I mistook the weird glimmer for a shadow cast by her swaying shoulders. I thought she was just reaching for the board to steady herself.

Then I saw her hands moving on the board and knew that a gravity panel was swinging open on the void! I leapt toward her with a warning cry.

If she heard me she gave no sign. You can hear a shout through a thin helmet, but she didn't even turn. She just darted sideways and then forward—straight through the panel into the utter black emptiness of space! A flash of light—and she was gone!

The panel closed so soundlessly you could have heard a pin drop.

I had trouble with my breath again. For an instant my throat had an iron brace around it. Then I remembered that she hadn't gone out unprotected into the void. Her suit would keep the cold out, and the magnetic suction disks on her wrists and knees would enable her to cling to the hull, to crawl along it. But if she'd gone out to do a repair job on the hull, she had the kind of courage you read about in the Admiralty Reports.

If I had it, it was glazed over with a thick coating of ice. I stood braced against the bulkhead, the old Adam in me chanting a hymn to life, a hymn to the Sun, and feeling glad I wasn't in her shoes.

What a way for a guy to feel!

Then something happened to me. I saw her face again, deep in my mind, and it seemed to be pleading with me. It wasn't just a pleading. There was music and wonder in it!

I could hear the pound of surf on a golden beach, and the sun was warming the sea and the air, and she was in my arms and I was kissing her.

Then it was night and the palms were bending lower over us, and the moonlight was so bright I could hardly see the web of radiance around her head. But I could hear the rise and fall of paddles, and someone singing far off over the water. We were running down the beach toward the pounding surf. Water was glistening on her tanned arms and I could hear her laughter.

Pete had leapt to his feet. He was staring at me, sweat standing out on his forehead in great, shining beads.

"What did I tell you, son?" he groaned. "A sickness of the mind—"

His voice thickened, broke.

The terror in his stare made me realize how close to the brink I was. His refusal to believe the evidence of his eyes was an attempt at rationalization, but it wasn't a good attempt.

He was assuming the worst, taking his own madness for granted.

I grabbed him by both shoulders. "You're as sane as I am!" I yelled, shaking him. "That girl was here when we took over! A stowaway! What's so crazy about that?"

Pete's throat moved as he swallowed. "Let go of me, Jim! Believe what you want! I'm going crazy—and tryin' to explain it won't stop it!"

"Common sense will stop it! Did you notice that vacuum suit she was wearing? It's as ancient as the ship! It must have come out of the ship's locker!"

Pete stared at me until I lost my head. "She's out on the hull alone! You hear? Alone, in a suit that won't give her much protection! If her irons slip she'll be done for! She's either stark staring mad or—"

My thoughts came so fast I had to stop. But my mind raced on. Was she actually mad? Or had she crawled out of hiding to find herself in a ship that was fast becoming a droning death trap?

A woman hiding in the dark, with her senses abnormally alert, would be quick to get the awful feel of a ship about to fly asunder. She wouldn't have to guess. She'd know!

A girl pilot? Well, why not? There were plenty of girl pilots working their fingers to the bone to earn passage money in Callisto City. Stowing away would be a short cut to freedom and the green hills of Earth. You couldn't blame a girl for hating the dust and roar of an atomic power plant, or the drudgery of a mining job.

I could picture her succumbing to blind panic, ripping a suit down from the locker, and crawling out into the void to tighten the gravity bolts on the naked hull with a magneto-wrench.

"Jeebies always try to kill themselves!" Pete croaked. "You get to pitying them! Your head swells and you get all choked up with pity! And that's when you know you've blown your top!"

I answered that with a voice that rang hard. "All right, have it your own way! She's a jeebie! But I'm not going to stand here pitying her! I'm going to help her!"

I never quite knew how I reached the locker, with imaginary eyes glittering at me from every corner of the ship. Pete's wild talk hadn't really shaken me. All loose talk about the mind is dangerous, of course. But I wasn't scared of anything I couldn't see.

The idea of a haunted ship seemed silly to me. Almost laughable. But I had to admit the ship had the feel of occupancy about it. I half expected that a second helmeted figure would pop out of the shadows before I could go to the aid of the first.

My palms were sweating as I struggled into a spacesuit that hadn't been occupied for at least a century. There were five suits hanging in the locker, and I picked the biggest one. It was a little too small for me, but I couldn't complain much on that score. It kinked a little, then drew tight over the shoulders, but nothing ripped when I moved.

I must have looked grotesque in that old, stiff, freakish garment, all bulges and creases. A big flaring dome over my head, feet like metal pancakes clattering on the deck.

But I wasn't concerned with my appearance, just my oxygen intake.

Back by the gravity panel, Pete tried desperately to stop me. His bony hands went out, plucked at my wrists. I couldn't hear him babbling outside the helmet. But I could see his shining eyes and moving lips. His eyes were tortured, pleading.

He might as well have been pleading with a man a hundred miles away—or a century dead!

I was deaf to reason. I was feeling merely a blind instinct to help a woman who had taken on a man's job.

Pete's eyes followed me as I went clumping toward the control board, and I felt a sudden tug of pity for him. If I never came back, he'd miss me a lot. Good old Pete! To make him feel better I flashed him a smile and waved him back.

"Sit down and relax, old-timer!" I said. "I'm just going out for a little breath of fresh air!"

It was just as well he couldn't hear me. He was real touchy about space. You had to treat it with respect. The lads who sailed the seas of Terra before Pete started reaching for the stars with his little pink hands had what it takes, and their lingo is the spaceman's lingo still. But to Pete spacemen were a notch higher in every respect. Nothing riled him more than loose talk about reading the weather by the glass or taking a squint at the North Star. Or going out for a breather on deck!

I thought of all that as I went out. Oh, Pete was a special character if ever there was one.

CHAPTER III

The Mirage Pup

I crawled out into the void on my hands and knees, clinging to the rough hull, digging with my magnetic irons into the thick coating of meteoric dust and grit and rubble the ship had picked up in deep space.

Brother, it's all yours if you want it! A wind that isn't a wind tearing at you; the stars blazing in a black pit, and a million light years staring you in the face, doing your thinking for you, warning you that forever is too long a time to go somersaulting through space shrouded in a blanket of ice.

You feel your grip slipping, know it can't slip, and dig, dig with your knees. You look up and there's the flame of a rocket jet missing you by inches. You look down and there's nothing to maim or sear you—just utter blackness. Believe me, that's worse!

I stared straight across the hull through a spiraling splotch of blue flame toward the stern rocket jets. The flame whorl came from diffuse matter friction. Tiny particles hit the ship, bounced off and set up an electrical discharge in the ether.

It's cool and it doesn't burn. If you keep your head you can crawl right through it.

I started crawling the instant I saw her. She was clinging to the hull between two flaring rocket jets, her magneto-wrench rising and falling in the unearthly glare.

A swaying figure wrapped in blue light, her face looking pinched and white and faraway through the globe on her shoulders. The helmet itself looked small against the vast backdrop of space. But as I crawled toward her it kept getting larger—like an expanding soap bubble. I had the crazy feeling that there was a big crowd down below, waiting to jeer or cheer!

I threw the illusion off and let my irons carry me back and forth in a crazy kind of jig. The magnetics had to be guided by my muscles and my will. It was twist and turn, go limp and brace hard, relax and edge forward.

Suddenly the ship lurched, giving off a blinding flare. I knew it was just a stress we'd hit—one of those little pockets in space where the diffuse matter of the void is sucked dry by energies that don't show up on the instruments.

Ships pass through stresses fast. But when the flare vanished I was dangling head downwards from the hull, my right knee attached to solid metal, the rest of me hugging empty space.

Furiously I slammed my left knee upward, twisted my body forward, and got a firm grip on the hull again with my wrist irons. It was a contortionist feat which brought the blood rushing to my ears. When my head stopped spinning I was staring into the face of the girl I'd risked my neck to save in an inferno of ice and flame.

We were so close our helmets almost touched. But she wasn't looking at me. Six feet from my swaying knees she was making frantic gestures with her magneto-wrench, her face a twisting mask of horror. Her body was twisting too and she seemed to be fighting off something I couldn't see!

Frantic with alarm, I strained forward and threw my right arm about her.

At least, I thought I did! But my iron-weighted wrist seemed to pass right through her! It whipped through emptiness to strike the hull with an impact that sent a stab of pain darting up my arm to my shoulder. The pain was agonizing for an instant; then it fell away.

At the same instant I saw the light. It was faint at first, a pale spectral glow that haloed her helmet and lapped in concentric waves about her knees. It wasn't a flame whorl. It gave off iridescent glints and grew swiftly brighter, turning from pale blue to dazzling azure. Then it became a weaving funnel of light that spurted from the hull with a low humming sound.

The humming was unearthly. It penetrated my helmet and became a shrill inward keening with a quality hard to define. Imagine a butterfly of sound struggling fiercely to escape from a sonic chrysalis. It was a little like that, a kind of shrill fluttering on the tonal plane.

The light did not remain attached to the hull. It shot up into the void and became a vertical shaft of downsweeping radiance. From its summit pulsing ripples ascended, giving it the aspect of a waterfall. Then it became a prism, flashing with all the colors of the spectrum.

A man may awaken from a nightmare, stare for an instant into the darkness and try to rationalize his fears. But this was no nightmare! As I stared up the iridescence was replaced by a leaf-screen effect shot through with crimson filaments. Shadows appeared amidst the ripples, straight and jagged lines of some tenuous substance that seemed to mold itself into a pattern.

It may have been imagination. But for the barest instant as I stared at the incredible shape of radiance a face seemed to look out at me. A fat face, bloated, toadlike, supported by a shadowy neck that swelled out beneath it like the hood of a rearing cobra!

Suddenly my scalp crawled and my helmet seemed to contract, pressing against my skull with a deadly firmness. An electrolube!

I knew instinctively that the flame shape was an electrolube—a devouring entity of the void which snaked through deep space close to Saturn's orbit, a whiplash shape of pure force with a hellish affinity for life, its negative charge seeking a positive charge with which to unite!

It was itself alive, the ultimate life form, sentient and polarized, an energy eater that sucked nourishment from electrical impulses.

And there was just enough positive electricity in the human body to give the horror the power to destroy by slashing down in swift, flesh-destroying stabs that could cut through a spacesuit like a knife through jelly!

Flesh and blood had no chance against it.

For one awful instant I looked straight into the eyes of a girl I couldn't save, an instant as long as a lifetime to the poor fool who loved her! No, I'm not raving! Do you think I'd have crawled out into the everlasting night of space if I hadn't known there could be no other woman for me?

I'd never have crawled out into that everlasting night of space for any other woman.

She didn't wait for the horror to slice down. She jerked her knees, tore her wrists free and shut her eyes. Then she was gone. She didn't even move her lips to say good-by. Space was her bridegroom. It took her and she was gone.

I looked away. Not caring how soon death came, knowing I'd be with her if I just stayed with the ship.

I waited for the anguish to hit me. I waited for a full minute. Two. I shut my eyes as she had done.

When I opened them the electrolube had vanished. And when I looked down, the void had grown brighter. Gone was the great ringed disk of Saturn.

Just little frosty stars glittered far-off, mocking. And another planet that was mottled pink and yellow. A ringless planet, swimming in a murky haze, with eleven little moons spinning around it—eight on one side, three on the other. One of the moons was red.

Jupiter is bigger than Saturn, bigger than a thousand Earths. And I was moving away from it on a droning ship's hull, a tiny fleck of matter of no importance in that awful sweep of space. But when I dragged myself back through the gravity panel into the ship my brain was bursting with a despair so vast it seemed to dwarf the vastness of space.

Pete was standing just inside the panel, holding something furry and black in his arms that squirmed in the cold light. When he saw me he uttered a smothered oath.

I tugged at my helmet, got it off.

"Jim, lad, I was afraid you was a goner!" Pete choked. "You went chasing mirages on the hull. Mirages, Jim!"

My jaw dropped. I stood stock still, staring at him, unable to believe my eyes.

"It's all my fault!" Pete groaned. "Me and my rantings! Jeebies my foot! Soon as you went out I got to thinkin'. There's a beastie could do it, a little black, furry beastie called a mirage pup!

"Sired on Pluto, breedin' on Pluto in the dark an' the cold! Squattin' on its haunches, projectin' thoughts! Makin' 'em look solid and real! Sounds too, though you don't hear the sounds with your ears!

"His memories, Jim! Things he's seen himself, long, long ago! We been makin' pets of 'em so long we take 'em for granted. All the old skippers had 'em on their ships."

"Oh, Eternity!" I choked.

"They can make thoughts look as solid as a cake of ice, Jim! Three-dimensional, like! I figured it this way. There was a girl, about a hundred years ago, took a ship—this ship—out to Saturn! And somethin' happened to the ship. So she went out to fix what was wrong and maybe never came back. Her gravity irons could have slipped—"

"No," I said quickly. "She let go deliberately because—it was better that way!"

I was staring at the little beast. Take a rabbit, puff it out, paint it black, and give it two huge, spectral, tarsierlike eyes! Give it a purple snout, devilishly long claws. Breed it with a full-blooded Scotch Terrier and you'll get—a Plutonian mirage pup!

The little beast whined, then yapped and wagged its tail at me. Its ear stood straight up. It nuzzled Pete's palm.

Mirage pups could coat everything over with evanescent images that looked real. They could change the outside as well as the inside of a ship. They could put Saturn beyond the viewpane, instead of Jupiter. Put a girl in the ship who lived once, engrave an image of that girl on your heart so that getting it off would mean a tearing anguish.

Yes, a mirage pup could do that because it would have a long memory. Mirage pups lived to a ripe old age. Slowed metabolism. The cold and dark of Pluto. Long periods of hibernation on that frigid planet while they dreamed the long, long dreams of their youth. And projected those dreams on awakening. Dreams, memories, buried loyalties.

If a master had been kind they'd never forgot! If a mistress had been kind—

The wetness at the corners of my eyes was making me blink.

So the mirage pup had followed her out on the hull, long ago. Crouched down perhaps, shivering, its paws covering its face. And the electrolube hadn't touched it! A small body, a small positive charge! No nourishment for an electrolube in a mirage pup!

Then it had crawled back, whining and hopeless and lost, back into the ship. Hibernation in a dark corner! For one hundred years!

"I found him in the tube room!" Pete grunted. "He was hidin' behind one o' the atomotors, coiled up like a porcupine. But I knew he was just playin' possum! I could see his eyes—blazin' out at me in the dark!"

"Yeah," I said, gruffly.

"You want to hold him, Jim?"

Pete extended the little beast toward me, but I shied away. I couldn't bear to touch anything that she had touched! Later, maybe, when I got over the shock.

"Guess we'll never know how the ship found its way to the graveyard!" Pete said. "Say, do you suppose if we're patient he'll project a picture of what happened? Maybe he'll start fillin' the tub with mirages again!"

"They only do it when they're scared!" I told him. "And lonely and miserable! He's not scared now! He likes us, worse luck!"

"He was homesick, eh?"

"That's right! For his past, for his mistress." I looked at Pete. "As for the ship, I can make a pretty good guess. Ship went into an orbit of its own, close to Saturn. It drifted around for about a century. Then a salvage crew found it and towed it to Callisto City to be sold as junk. It has happened before, plenty of times!"

"Never with a mirage pup inside, I bet!"

"Maybe not!"

I turned away, feeling all hollow inside, like one of those caterpillars that pupae wasps sting to death and feast on until they're nothing but husks. Grave bait, lying in a tunnel deep in the earth.

I knew the only chance I had of crawling out of the tunnel into the sunlight again was to give the little beast a kick. If he got lonely and frightened, he'd see her again! He'd start dreaming about her, and she'd come to life again, as a memory in the brain of a mirage pup!

But I never could be that cruel.

"What's the matter, Jim?" Pete asked, concerned. "You look sick!"

I wheeled on him. "I didn't tell you what happened outside. If you open your trap again—I will!"

Pete avoided my eyes. "I didn't ask you, Jim!"

I knew then that the pup had projected two sets of images, one in the control room for Pete's benefit and one outside for me to live through. A mirage pup could generate images like an electronic circuit, duplicate them in all directions, pile them up in layers. Automatically without thinking, to ease its own wretchedness.

Pete had been able to follow me as I crawled along the hull. He knew what I was going through.

I moved away from him, sat down on the chronometer and cradled my head in my arms.

Dusk.

Dawn.

Dusk.

Dawn.

You don't see the sun rise and set inside a spaceship, but that's how the days seem to pass. Your mind grows a little darker when it's time for the sun to set on Earth. Lightens when it rises.

Dusk. Dawn. Dusk. Dawn. Three days. Four. But for me it was just dusk. My mind didn't lighten at all.

How does it feel to love a woman a century dead? If you'd asked me, I couldn't have told you. Because she wasn't dead to me. I kept seeing her pale, beautiful face and everywhere I turned time seemed to stretch away into endless vistas. If I'd been on Earth, in New York or Chicago, I could have gone out and lost myself in the crowds and the glitter. But it wouldn't have helped.

I turned and looked at the sleeping mirage pup. He lay on my bunk with his legs coiled up under him, his moist nose resting on his folded forelimbs. He looked like a prize puppy at a pet show, but what a puppy!

In his unfathomable animal mind was that strange capacity for projecting illusions, of making them seem three-dimensional and real. He could blur the viewpane, fill it with unreal star fields, draw shapes of energy from the void.

But he couldn't change his memories by slicklying them over with the pale cast of thought! At bottom he was just a dumb beast. He had the mind of a puppy, a mind that chased fantasms while asleep through a labyrinth of dark alleyways. He twitched and shook while asleep, just like an excitable mutt.

Little agitated noises came from him. His nostrils quivered, his tail vibrated and he rolled over in his sleep and started scratching himself. Thump. Thump. Thump.

What was he thinking about? A girl in a garden with the moonlight in her hair? Stooping to pat him or feeding him yummies? He'd rolled over and was lying with his forelimbs stretched straight out, as though he were reaching for the moon.

But I knew he wasn't seeing the moon. He was reaching for something I couldn't see or hear or touch, something older than the human race maybe.

I was hating him furiously when Pete came into the compartment. He grabbed my arm and started shaking me.

"Jim! Jim, lad! Get a grip on yourself! We'll be hittin' the Heaviside in a minute!"

"What do I care?" I lashed out. "Go away, can't you? Blow!"

"Now, now, son!" he pleaded. "That's no way to act! You can't bring her back! And if you keep eatin' your heart out—"

"Get out!" I shouted, heaving myself from the bunk. "Get out—*get out!*"

"Don't be a fool, Jim! You've got to get rid of that grievin' look! The skyport Johnnies are funny that way! You walk out of this ship with your eyes burnin' holes in your face, and they'll think you got somethin' to hide!

"Look at yourself in a mirror! Whiskers sproutin' out of your chin, face sooty as a tube fittin' and no fight left in you! You got to get back the look of a fightin' fury, son! A lad who can stand up to a port clearance inspector and say 'Me an' my buddy, here, we're headin' for that gate, and if you want to stay healthy—'"

"What?"

"Jehoshaphat!" Pete groaned. "He don't even hear me!"

I stood up. "Okay, Pete!" I told him. "I heard you! Most of it, anyway. And I'll get myself spruced up. How close are we to the Heaviside?"

He heaved a high sigh of relief. "We'll hit it in half an hour, Jim!"

He grinned. "He's got to have a harness, Jim. I'll rig up a harness for him!"

CHAPTER IV

New York Kid

We made as good a landing as could be expected, considering the way my hands shook when I brought her down.

Right smack in the middle of La Guardia field! It's the biggest skyport in the System, and you can't miss it if you're a New York kid, with the lay of the land and the navigation lights burned into your brain from boyhood.

One of my own ancestors had brought a primitive skyplane down on that field during the Second World War, when the First Atomic Age was just starting.

They'd built the field up quite a bit in the intervening years—built it in revolving stations toward the Heaviside. You could make contact with the atomic clearance floats at sixty-five miles, and pick up a guiding beam from a rocket glider twenty miles above the grounded runways.

But you can't build the past out of existence. There were ghosts all over that field, grease monkeys in khaki jeans, and taking care of jet planes that had passed into limbo before the first space crate took off for Mars. At least, that's the way Pete seemed to feel, and I could sympathize with his screwball occultism.

I had a feeling that my own ancestor was down there, shading his eyes, watching me make a perfect twenty-point landing. His eyes shining with pride because I made such a good job of bringing her in. What he didn't know wouldn't hurt him.

I thought we'd have trouble with the clearance officials, but when I came striding out of the gravity port with the mirage pup clinging to my right shoulder I was greeted with nothing but merriment. Tickle a man's sense of humor if you want him to do you a favor!

Just seeing that crazy little beast put everyone in the best of humor. A tall, young-old lad with puckered brows and graying hair, his skin bleached by irradiation particles, took one swift look at my pilot's license, ignored Pete's jittery stare, and gave the mirage pup a pat that set his tail wagging.

"What's his name?" somebody asked.

I thought fast. "Flipover!" I said.

"Boy, he's quite a pup! Cute! Don't see many of them since the new quarantine regulations went into effect. They have to be defleaed too often!"

"All the little critters jumped off him in deep space!" I said.

The officer chuckled. "Okay, my friend! You can pass through. The first gate on your right!"

We were through the gate and ascending a ramp toward a skyline that brought a lump to my throat in less time than you could say, "Flip Flipover!"

Little old New York hadn't changed much in ten years. The white terrific flare that spiraled up from its heart was as bright as the day I'd first seen it. Broadway—and a New York kid is hooked for life. He'll always come back to it.

But now I didn't want to head for the bright lights. I wanted to find a lodging close to the harbor lights, where I could look out over the bay at night and—remember things. Her face just before she let go, not really seeing me. Her eyes—

Pete was shaking his arm. "Set him down, Jim! Put him into that harness I rigged up. Give him a chance to stretch his legs!"

"Sure, why not?" I grunted.

I set Flipover down on the ramp, fitted Pete's makeshift harness to his shoulders, and wrapped the leash-end around my wrist.

The little beast started tugging right off.

"Looks like he knows his way around!" Pete chuckled. "Maybe New York was his home town!"

That didn't sound funny to me. But a few minutes later I was taking it seriously. The crazy pup had led us deep into the labyrinth of dark streets which bordered the skyport, and there was no stopping him. I had all I could do to keep up with him.

Pete's eyes were shining with excitement. "Give him his head!" he urged.

"What do you think I'm doing?" I yelled.

From the houses lights streamed out. Cornerset windows flamed in the dusk and people moved across shadowed panes. Music came from beyond the windows, loud, tumultuous. Someone was playing Milhaud's Bal Martiniquais on an old-fashioned percussion instrument with shallow keys.

I liked it. Give me color in music, polychromes. Give me color in life. The flare of rocket jets, the blackness of space, a spinning wheel in a big crystal casino—

I'd stay one week on Earth! Then I'd be off again and never come back. I'd bury myself in the farthest—

"Give him his head!" Pete yelled.

Flipover had swerved and was heading for a narrow walk leading to a fairly large circular house surrounded by a garden plot bright with yellow flowers. There was a fountain in the middle of the garden and it was sending up jets of spray which drenched Flipover as he tore down the path.

I almost let go of the leash as I played it out. The house had the look of age about it but not of neglect. We were within thirty feet of it when the front door banged open and a big, angry-faced man came striding out.

Down the path he came, straight toward me. A sunbronzed giant of a lad built like a cargo wrestler, but with keen, probing eyes behind glasses that had slipped far down on his nose.

When he saw me he stopped dead. Then he adjusted his glasses and peered at me wordlessly, his hands knotting into fists.

Flipover was straining furiously, but I drew him in quickly and returned the big lug's stare.

"So you're the guy!" he roared.

It happened so quickly I was taken by surprise. His fist lashed out, caught me on the jaw.

I felt Flipover tear loose as I went crashing backwards, my head filled with forked lightning.

He jumped me the instant I hit the ground. About three tons of flailing weight crashed down on my shoulders, pinning me to the walk.

As deliberately as I could, I raised my right knee, whammed it into his stomach and threw one arm about his neck in a strangle lock he couldn't break.

"That's showin' him, son!" I heard Pete yell.

I tried not to break his glasses. But I had to be a little rough because he wanted to play rough.

About one minute later he was standing in the fountain, eying me angrily from behind a rising curtain of spray. The water came to his knees.

Suddenly his lips split in a grin. He threw back his head and roared with laughter. "By George, you sure know how to cool off a hot-head!"

"Well—thanks!" I said, modestly.

He stepped out of the fountain, walked up to me and thrust out his hand. "Phillip Goddard's the name!" he said. "She just gave me my ring back! When she said she couldn't marry a certified public accountant I knew there was someone else. You're the kind of lad her great-grandmother went for—and she's just like that famous ancestor of hers!"

"Ancestor?" I gulped.

He nodded. "Just like her! Pluckiest girl in the System! Back in the First Atomic Age it was. First girl pilot to make a solo hop to Saturn—"

His face darkened. "Something happened to her! She never came back. But she's come alive again in her granddaughter! No indoor cookie for Anne Haven's granddaughter! I'm not exactly a lightweight, but I make my living adding up long rows of figures. If she married me what would be the result?"

The grin returned to his face. "She'd pine away from boredom. I like it. I enjoy it! But the girl for me will have to be a red-headed adding machine."

He stepped back. "When I saw you coming up the walk I lost my head! Sour grapes, fella! If I couldn't have her—I didn't intend to step aside for a rival without putting up a fight! Little boy stuff! I had no call to take a sock at you! You're all right, fella!"

He gave me a resounding thump on the back. "So the best man gets her! Okay, I can be a good loser! I don't know how long you've known her, but I bet if you pop the question tonight, when she has that faraway look in her eyes again—"

"He never bets!" Pete cut in.

I didn't wait to thank him. I was running up the walk toward the house before he could let out a startled grunt. But I heard the grunt—far off in the darkness.

Then a door slammed and I was standing in a brightly lighted living room staring at her. A log fire was crackling in the grate and there was a big, framed painting in oils hanging on the wall, facing the entrance hall.

She was standing directly before the painting, staring down at Flipover. Flipover was wagging his tail and pawing at her knees, and she was stooping and patting him on the head. Only—she wasn't calling him by the name I had given him. She was calling him, "Tow Tow."

"Oh, I can't believe it! I can't, I can't. Granny's pup! You've come home, Tow Tow—and you are Tow Tow! I'd know you anywhere! You precious darling."

Then I saw the girl in the painting. She was wearing a space suit a hundred years out of date, and her hand was on the head of a mirage pup too. Only it was a mirage pup in oils! Life-sized, lifelike and unmistakably Tow Tow! The pup in the painting had the same dumb-bright unweaned look about him! Any child brought up with that painting before her would know the real Tow Tow when he came bounding home! He was like no other pup!

The girl who was patting the real Tow Tow raised her head suddenly, and looked at me!

For a full minute we just stood there, staring at each other. I don't know how she felt, but I knew how I felt! A family resemblance can be a remarkable thing! The contours of a face, the way the eyes look at you, and the trembling of lips shaped in a certain way can—make the universe reel!

Especially when there's no difference at all between the face of a girl a century dead and a living face you'd never thought to see again!

"Who are you?" she whispered.

I told her.

Her eyes were shining when I stopped telling her about myself. She swayed a little, and I think we both knew then how it was going to be.

She was in my arms before I realized that I didn't even know her name.

"It's Barbara!" she whispered, when I got around to asking her. That was quite a few minutes after I'd met her. You can't kiss a girl and ask her name in the same breath. And there was just a chance she'd be offended and refuse to tell me.

But Barbara was a darned good sport about it!

"I've never been kissed by a total stranger before!" she said. "Jim, it was wonderful!"

It sure was. We went back to it again.

It's been a long time, now. Seven years. And if I haven't proved you can fall in love with the same woman twice I've been living a lie. But I know that it isn't so. If I was living a lie, Tow Tow would be unhappy, and he'd be filling the house with mirages. But my five-year-old son, Bobby, isn't a mirage, and neither is the girl I married.

Sometimes, when I see the lights of the skyport through a cornerset window, and winds howl in from the bay, I get to wondering about Pete.

You see, he never came in that night, never joined us! He may have looked in through a window, and realized I'd reached my last "port o' call," a quiet harbor in a storm that had died away forever. He may have turned and gone stumbling off into the night!

I'll never know, of course. Good old Pete! Sometimes I get to thinking. A mirage pup can coil up in an old ship and hibernate for a century. Could a human being do that?

There are strange influences in deep space. Are there discharges in the electromagnetic field that could slow up the metabolism of a tired little character like Pete?

That's nonsense, of course.

I'll have to go now. Bobby's calling me. He's standing at the head of the stairs, in his pajamas, and he's waiting for me to tell him a bedtime story about what it's like out in the mighty dark.

"Pop, you promised! Aw, come on, Pop—"

I'll have to keep it simple, of course. But maybe tonight I'll tell him about Pete.

Maybe when he grows up he'll meet Pete.

Who knows?

———————

www.ingramcontent.com/pod-product-compliance
Ingram Content Group UK Ltd.
Pitfield, Milton Keynes, MK11 3LW, UK
UKHW031339260325
456749UK00002B/292

9 789366 382449